I0795472

GREAT SPORTS RIVALRIES

THE BOSTON BRUINS

Jamie Fickett

VS.

THE MONTREAL CANADIENS

A Stingray Book

SEAHORSE PUBLISHING

Teaching Tips for Caregivers and Teachers:

This Hi-Lo book features high-interest subject matter that will appeal to all readers in intermediate and middle school grades. It may be enjoyed by students reading at or above grade level as well as by those who are looking for age-appropriate themes matched with a less challenging reading level. Hi-Lo books are ideal for ELL readers, too.

Each book appeals to a striving reader's age and maturity level. Opportunities are provided for students to read words they already know while encountering a limited number of new, high-interest vocabulary words. With these supports in place, students will read more fluently while increasing reading comprehension. Use the following suggestions to help students grow as readers.

- Encourage the student to read independently at home.
- Encourage the student to practice reading aloud.
- Encourage activities that require reading.
- Establish a regular reading time.
- Have the student write questions about what they read.

Teaching Tips for Teachers:

Before Reading

- Ask, "What do I know about this topic?"
- Ask, "What do I want to learn about this topic?"

During Reading

- Ask, "What is the author trying to teach me?"
- Ask, "How is this like something I already know?"

After Reading

- Discuss how the text features (headings, index, etc.) help with understanding the topic.
- Ask, "What interesting or fun fact did you learn?"

TABLE OF CONTENTS

ENEMIES ON ICE

Some of the best hockey players of all time have played for the Boston Bruins and the Montreal Canadiens.

But these two NHL (National Hockey League) teams don't like each other very much. Their fierce **rivalry** is legendary.

The teams have played at least 744 games. Of those games, Montreal won 363 while Boston won 278. There were 103 ties.

FUN FACT

Montreal is in the country of Canada. Boston is in the U.S. state of Massachusetts. The two northern cities share a love of ice hockey.

CCM
WARR

1920s: THE RIVALRY BEGINS

The first matchup between the two teams came in 1925. The Bruins won 3 to 2 over the Canadiens.

In the 1929 semifinals, Boston won three **shutout** games in a row over Montreal. The Bruins went on to win the Stanley Cup.

FUN FACT

The Stanley Cup is awarded each year to the NHL Champion. The famous cup was donated by Sir Frederick Arthur Stanley in 1892.

1943: COMPETITIVE CANADIENS

In the early 1940s, the Canadiens were at the bottom of the NHL rankings. That all changed in 1943. The Habs had young stars and a bright future.

But the Bruins also had plenty of talent. They beat the Habs in a five-game series in the 1943 semifinals.

FUN FACT

The Canadiens nickname Habs may come from the French phrase **les habitants*****, which means "settlers."***

Bruins
N.H.L.
C
B

1952: HOSPITAL-BOUND

Maurice Richard

In 1952, the Bruins and the Habs met in the semifinals. It all came down to game 7.

The score was 1 to 1. Canadiens star Maurice "The Rocket" Richard had a head-on **collision** with Bruins player Leo Labine.

The Rocket was knocked flat on his back. Dazed and injured, he was escorted off the ice.

The Rocket went to the hospital, but not before he convinced the coach to put him back in at the end of the tied game. Half-conscious, he received the puck and scored the series-winning goal.

1958: A DYNASTY

From 1953 to 1969, the Canadiens won so often that people said they were a **dynasty**. They won the Stanley Cup ten times.

In the final game of the 1958 Stanley Cup series, Montreal had a 4 to 1 lead. But the Bruins scored two goals in the third period. The score was 4 to 3.

With one minute left, Montreal **defenseman** Doug Harvey scored. The Bruins hopes of a comeback were over.

FUN FACT

Doug Harvey was a master of controlling the puck. He revolutionized the way the defenseman position is played.

Doug Harvey

1971: GOALTENDER GREATNESS

Ken Dryden

In 1971, the Boston Bruins had legendary players Bobby Orr and Phil Esposito. They seemed guaranteed to win the NHL Championship.

But the Canadiens had other plans. In the final game of the quarterfinals, unknown Habs goaltender Ken Dryden saved almost every shot that Esposito made. Esposito said that Dryden had "arms like a giraffe."

FUN FACT

Ken Dryden was tall and lanky. He was known as "the four-story goalie."

1979: PENALTY

In the 1979 season, the Boston Bruins had another great team.

They met Montreal in the semifinals. In game 7, Boston was up 4 to 3. Then came a costly **penalty**. The Bruins had too many men on the ice.

Star Habs player Guy Lafleur was able to tie the score. In overtime, Yvon Lambert scored the series-winning goal for Montreal.

FUN FACT

Guy Lafleur is the all-time points leader in the history of the Canadiens.

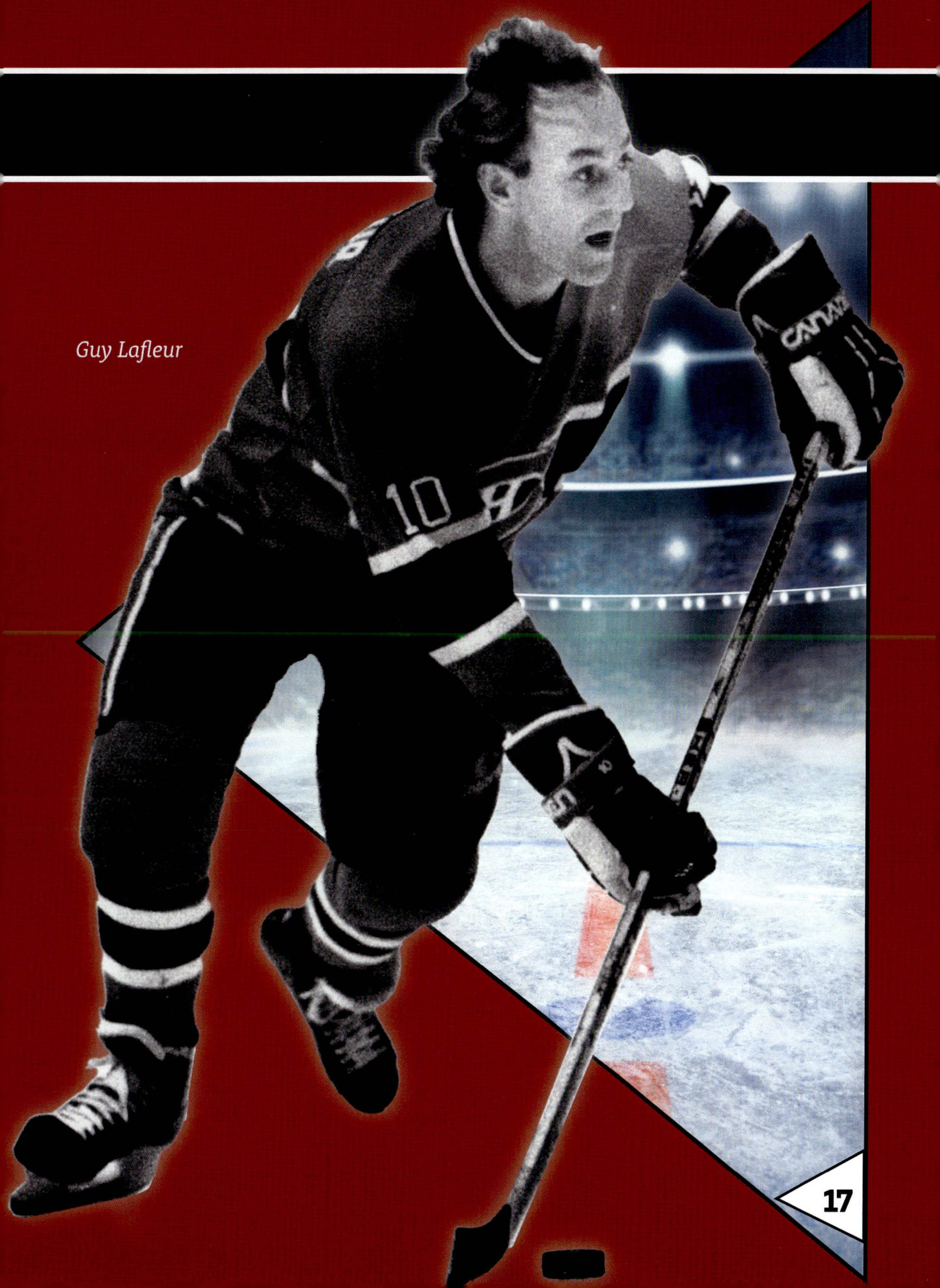

Guy Lafleur

1980s AND 1990s: ROY vs. NEELY

In the mid-1980s, Canadiens player Patrick Roy became one of the best goaltenders in the history of the sport.

Only one team was able to score regularly on "Saint Patrick." That was the Bruins.

From 1988 to 1994, Bruins player Cam Neely was Patrick Roy's ultimate **nemesis**. Somehow, Neely found a way to get the puck past Roy.

FUN FACT

Patrick Roy was known for talking to his goalposts throughout the game.

THE RIVALRY CONTINUES

Talented new players continue the **epic** rivalry between the Boston Bruins and the Montreal Canadiens.

Boston wingers David Pastrnak and Brad Marchand play against a Montreal defense led by Kaiden Guhle and Lane Hutson.

Who will win the next battle between these two great teams?

FUN FACT

In the 2023–2024 season, Bruins left wing Danton Heinen led a 9 to 4 blowout over Montreal.

GLOSSARY

collision (kuh-LIZH-uhn): a sudden and violent striking together of two people or objects

defenseman (di-FENS-man): a defensive player in hockey whose job is to protect their team's goal and get the puck to their teammates

dynasty (DYE-nuh-stee): a team that dominates their sport for a long time

epic (EP-ik): amazing or impressive

nemesis (NEM-uh-sis): an opponent whom you constantly struggle to defeat; an arch enemy

penalty (PEN-uhl-tee): a disadvantage or punishment that a team or player suffers for breaking the rules

rivalry (RYE-vuhl-ree): a longstanding, competitive, up-and-down relationship between two teams

shutout (SHUHT-out): a game in which one team fails to score

INDEX

AFTER READING QUESTIONS

1. Which of the rivals has won more games against the other?
2. What player was called "The Rocket"?
3. What was special about Ken Dryden's goaltending?
4. Who were the star players of the 1971 Boston Bruins?
5. Describe the relationship between Patrick Roy and Cam Neely.

ABOUT THE AUTHOR

Jamie Fickett lives in Long Island, New York. He enjoys sports, especially baseball. He likes to go to Mets games to watch his favorite player, Pete Alonso, play. He also enjoys cooking his famous chili and watching Formula 1 racing.

Written by: Jamie Fickett
Design by: Kathy Walsh
Editor: Kim Thompson

Library of Congress PCN Data
The Boston Bruins vs. The Montreal Canadiens
/Jamie Fickett
Great Sports Rivalries
ISBN 979-8-8873-5950-2 (hard cover)
ISBN 979-8-8873-5989-2 (paperback)
ISBN 979-8-8904-2048-0 (EPUB)
ISBN 979-8-8904-2107-4 (eBook)
Library of Congress Control Number: 2023912504

Printed in the United States of America.

Photographs/Shutterstock/Newscom: Cover: Bill Greenblatt, Archie Carpenter; p 5, 6, 9, 10, 13, 14, 17, 18, 21: Igor Link; p 5: Eric Canha; p 6: Anthony Nesmith; p 9: IHA/Icon SMI; p 10: @Wiki; p 13: Bildbyran; p 14: IHA/Icon SMI via Newscom; p 17: John Mahler; p 18: Eric Canha; p 21: David Kirouac/Icon Sportswire, Archie Carpenter

Seahorse Publishing Company
www.seahorsepub.com

Copyright © 2025 **SEAHORSE PUBLISHING COMPANY**

All rights reserved. No part of this publication may be reproduced, stored in a retrieval system or be transmitted in any form or by any means, electronic, mechanical, photocopying, recording, or otherwise, without the prior written permission of Seahorse Publishing Company.

Published in the United States
Seahorse Publishing
PO Box 771325
Coral Springs, FL 33077

SEAHORSE PUBLISHING